CW00531540

Out & About

In

Robin Hood Country

Janet Roberts

Tourist Information Centres

NEWARK
The Gilstrap Centre
Castlegate
Newark
Notts NG24 1BG
Tel: 01636 655765

NOTTINGHAM (SMITHY ROW)
1-4 Smithy Row
Nottingham NG1 2BY
Tel: 0115 915 5330

NOTTINGHAM (WEST BRIDGFORD)
County Hall
Loughborough Road
West Bridgford Notts NG2 7QP
Tel: 0115 977 3558

OLLERTON
Sherwood Heath
Ollerton Roundabout, Ollerton,
Nr Newark Notts NG22 9DR
Tel: 01623 824545

RETFORD
40 Grove Street
Retford
Notts DN22 6LD
Tel: 01777 860780

WORKSOP
Worksop Library
Memorial Avenue
Worksop Notts S80 2BP
Tel: 01909 501148

Contents

Robin Hood Theatre
Averham

SK766545
3 miles west of Newark off A617

Surely few villages the size of Averham (population less than 200) can boast of having their own thriving theatre.

It came about because of the Rev. Cyril Walker, who became Rector of Averham and Kelham in 1907. Cyril had been active in the Oxford Dramatic Society and soon founded an Operatic Society in the parish, acting as both Stage Manager and leading actor.

In 1913 he designed and with village carpenter Robert Lee and local volunteers, built a 150 seat theatre complete with ornate proscenium arch and flanked by plaster work. He called it the 'Robin Hood Opera House' and the new Theatre was filled every night, but due to the initial cost only showed a profit of one shilling and six pence (7p in decimal coinage!). Productions helped to keep spirits up during the Great War, and twice Donald Wolfit, then a keen Newark schoolboy, had small parts, including being a donkey! After becoming one of the country's finest Shakespearian actors, Sir Donald was knighted in 1957 for his services to the British Theatre.

In 1942 the Rev Cyril Walker died, and with him the enthusiasm for the theatre, and by 1951 it was closed. However a decade later the Rev. Mark Way organised a meeting to discuss the future of the Theatre building. It resulted in Valerie Baker of Gamston being offered a 7-year lease at a peppercorn rent of £1 a year to re-establish and reopen the Theatre. A Theatre Appeal Fund was opened with a personal donation of £300 from Valerie Baker and her husband. The target of at least £700 was soon surpassed due to the generosity of people in Newark and the surrounding area, and the personal support of the Wolfits.

At the Official Opening Ceremony in July 1961, Sir Donald and Lady Wolfit gave a Shakespearean Recital, including an Ode he had composed for the occasion, which started:

> *Artistic creation they say knows no bounds,*
> *Now a cleric named Walker who rode to the hounds*
> *Could preach a good sermon, and painted fine scenery,*
> *Bethought him of Sherwood and also its greenery.*
> *So he hired him a carpenter; splendid and good,*
> *And built him a theatre, he called Robin Hood.*
> *Then out from the village and town, harum-scarum,*
> *Came actors and audience converging on Averham.*

In 1967 the lease of the Theatre was renegotiated by Valerie Baker and bought by Sir Donald Wolfit for £1,000. He then handed the theatre over to a Trust administered by himself, Valerie Baker and the Bishop of Sherwood.

An Appeal Fund for £5,000 was opened and alterations were nearing completion when Sir Donald Wolfit died suddenly in 1968. Lady Wolfit succeeded him as a trustee.

The theatre soon established regional and national links for drama students, and such people as Simon Ward, Isla Blair and Christopher Timothy began their careers at the Robin Hood.

Following the retirement of Valerie Baker and the appointment of Mrs Jose King as Director, negotiations started regarding the theatres long-term future. In 1980 Nottinghamshire County Council took over the trusteeship.

The theatre continues to uphold its national reputation with many well-known actors having appeared there, amongst them: Cecil Day Lewis; Michael Dennison; Dulcie Gray, Judi Dench; Anthony Hopkins and Geraldine McEwan.

There are bar and coffee areas and an attractive supper room seating about 60, with the theatre's own caterers providing before and after performance meals. There is wheelchair access.

For further information:
Contact Tourist Info.

Models of the Mayflower

All Saints Church, Babworth SK688809

2 miles west of Retford A620

A stunning model of the sailing ship The Mayflower occupies the wall between two of the windows in the medieval church of All Saints, Babworth. The model is made of dried flowers, and in springtime birds like to fly into the church and steal the material for their nests! It commemorates the fact that the parson, Richard Clyfton, together with Scrooby postmaster William Brewster, formed a Separatists movement in the 16th Century. They wanted greater freedom of worship and religious tolerance, believing that the fledgling Church of England should abandon all Roman Catholic-style ritual and conduct services devoted to pure worship. These views were considered so outrageous and illegal, that the Separatists' very lives were in danger. In 1605, they had to leave their homes and possessions and flee to Holland. Richard Clyfton was to die in Amsterdam in 1616 but due to social and political pressure there, the remainder of the group decided to head to America, sailing on the Mayflower in 1620.

The new colony they formed was called Plimoth - now modern Plymouth, Massachusetts. To celebrate their first harvest the Pilgrims enjoyed a feast of cod, seabass and wildfowl - a far cry from the deprivations of their voyage. Thanksgiving Day is now celebrated annually by millions of Americans.

The Church also contains an artist's impression of the arrival of the Pilgrim Fathers in America. An inmate of nearby Ranby Prison, using an old blackboard, painted it. The figures are wearing bright colours, for Separatists did not believe in the austere costume of the Puritans.

There is another detailed scale mode of the Mayflower, constructed from 14,000 matchsticks, which stands near the altar. This also was made by a prisoner at Ranby.

All Saints Church stands at the end of a tree-lined track in a quiet wooded glade. At the end of January it is a mass of snowdrops, replaced then by primroses. They in turn are superseded by a sea of bluebells.

The Mayflower Trail - a circular tour of 38-40 miles visiting the historic villages and sites of Pilgrim Father's Country, in North Nottinghamshire.

Contact Tourist Information Centre

Rocking Ceremony

Blidworth Sk587555

7 miles east of Mansfield A617, then B6020

This ceremony is held annually on the first Sunday in February at St Mary of the Purification, Blidworth. The 2nd February is the date of the celebration of the purification of Mary following childbirth and of the Presentation of the infant Jesus in the Temple.

A male baby who was born nearest to Christmas Day and whose parents are resident in Blidworth is Baptized in the morning of the Rocking Ceremony, and in the afternoon is blessed and rocked in a 100-year old wooden cradle which has been decorated with flowers. The child receives a Bible for his later use and a Register of Rockings is fixed to the wall in the Baptistry.

The Rocking Ceremony goes back to medieval times, but it fell into disuse in the 19th century and was revived again in 1922 by local Vicar, the Rev. John Lowndes. In its original form, it appears to have been a short play, depicting the Presentation of Jesus. Today it takes the form of a service held in the Parish Church of Blidworth and still retaining the theme of Presentation of the Infant.

The church at Blidworth would have originally been a wooden structure, but was replaced by one of stone during the Saxon period. It was known as the Chapel of St Lawrence until the time of Richard III (1483 - 1485), when a tower was built onto 'The church of St Mary'.

The tower is the only remaining part of the old church, as the original structure fell down in 1736, after being in a 'bad state of repair' for some time. Rhodes of Barlborough carried out the rebuilding work, and the arcade of five arches was supposedly the design of a pupil of Christopher Wren. The repaired church was re-opened in 1740, and the church was further enlarged in 1839.

Blidworth is frequently referred to in connection with Robin Hood. Maid Marian is said to have lived in the parish prior to her marriage, and Will Scarlett is reputedly buried in Blidworth churchyard.

Whilst these claims may be disputed, a model stone church similar, if not an exact replica of St Mary's is in the graveyard. William Tansley, a local builder, gave it to the church in 1963. His next-door neighbour, Mr Cutmore made the windows.

Mulberries Coffee Shop

SK659449

1 mile from junction A6097 and A612 at Bulcote near Burton Joyce

Situated within Tall Trees Garden Centre is a little refreshment centre specializing in teas and coffees. They have over 180 varieties, with coffees from nine different areas of the world, as well as flavoured ones such as chocolate orange and French vanilla.

There is a small cafè area with a helpful, informative staff and a packed menu listing such things as:-

'Mulberries Spiced Infusion. Tastes like a liquid Christmas Cake made from orange, cinnamon, cloves, raisins and hibiscus flowers. A great caffeine-free winter warmer.'

'Assan Harmutty T.G.F.O.P. Generally the more letters that a tea name has, the higher the quality. These letters stand for Tippy, Golden Flowery, Orange Pekoe.'

After sampling the various beverages it is possible to purchase larger quantities to take home, and Mulberries also runs a Mail Order service throughout Britain and Europe.

In addition to all the teas and coffees there is a large selection of home made cakes, as Mulberries claims to use over 100 recipes.

Outside a pair of peacocks guard the well-stocked nursery that carries a large selection of orchids, cacti and tropical houseplants, and well as one of the biggest collections of terracotta pots in Nottingham. Specimen plants are their speciality, and not surprisingly, tall trees are in abundance.

Mulberries is open between 9am and 6 pm daily

Email
mulbscoffeeshop@aol.com

Painted Murals

St Peter's Church
Clayworth

SK725885
7 miles northeast of Retford
on the B1403

The renowned Scottish artist Phoebe Anna Traquair heavily decorated the chancel of this ancient church with fine murals in 1905. She is considered a leading artist of the Arts and Crafts movement in Scotland at the turn of the last century. In addition to murals she used her artistic skill to produce paintings, book bindings, jewellery, enamelling, embroidery, manuscript illumination and lettering. She exhibited in Chicago, London, Turin and St Louis.

She was the first woman to be elected an honorary member of the Royal Scottish Academy, was also a member of the Edinburgh Arts and Crafts Club, the Guild of Woman Binders and the Royal Society of Painters in Water Colours.

The murals at Clayworth were part of five mural schemes, her most famous being Mansfield Place Church, Edinburgh, once a Catholic Church and now run by the Mansfield Traquair Trust.

Phoebe Anna Traquair responded to the location and the moment rather than work out all the details in advance so few sketches of her design work exist. She let the design idea form in her mind, and then drew directly onto the walls using chalk. She then worked in oil paints diluted with turpentine, which when applied to the dry, white-painted plaster surface, gave a translucency similar to that of watercolour painting onto paper. The final beeswax coating was applied by hand to give a silky soft sheen and to protect the paint from the climate.

This publicity photograph of her taken about 1897 shows her chalking an outline of her composition directly on to a wall.

Phoebe Anna Traquair frequently depicted the faces of friends and admirers into her work. At St. Peter's some of the children in one of the murals attended the church at that time.

Behind the altar is an Arabesque border of the (True) Vine with small singing angels.

Elizabeth Hirst, an internationally acclaimed art restorer, renovated the murals to their original splendour during1996.

The square tower of St Peter's, with its pinnacles and eight quaint gargoyles dates from early in the 12th century, and in parts probably from pre-Conquest times. Sections of the wall between the nave and chancel are equally old and have herringbone masonry near the arch.

Underneath one of the Norman pillars, and nearly hidden underneath the pew seat, is a tiny recumbent figure, perhaps the memorial to the child of the stonemason - nobody knows.

A 'Nodding Donkey'

Duke's Wood, Eakring

SK 677602

10 miles west Newark A617 signed Eakring

Serious searches for oil in Britain started during World War I but were largely unsuccessful. Then in 1934, BP launched a major exploration programme and oil-bearing sandstone was found near Eakring in June 1939. By 1941 the Duke's Wood site was being developed, as by then oil was the key to victory in the raging global conflict. Without oil no vehicles, ships, or planes could move, and as our supplies all came from the Middle East, the German U-boats, preying in wolf packs, targeted tankers, and bombing raids in dock areas destroyed almost a million barrels.

Britain's Secretary of Petroleum, Geoffrey Lloyd, called an emergency meeting in London in August 1942 to discuss the crisis. It was decided that D'Arcy Exploration Company, a subsidiary of the Anglo Iranian Oil Company (now BP) should develop Britain's own oil fields to their full potential.

At that time 50 producing wells had been completed at Eakring ranging in depth from 2,380 to 2,500 feet, yielding half a million barrels of high grade crude oil a year. Development had been slow mainly because the thirteen large rigs were designed for deep drilling in Persia (Iran). These rigs took two weeks to build and two weeks to dismantle and move to the next location.

It was decided that modern American rotary jack knife rigs would be more appropriate, since the aim was to drill an additional 100 wells in the Duke's Wood area. These rigs only took one day to erect and one day to dismantle.

Consequently C. Southwell, an industry representative with 20 years' experience with the D'Arcy Company, was dispatched to America on September 3rd 1942. Talks in Washington went well, but American legislation was such that the purchase of equipment could not be issued to foreign corporations or foreign governments.

After two months of urgent discussion a solution was reached. A contract was drawn up between D'Arcy and the American oil companies Noble and Porter. The latter would purchase the equipment and employ the drilling crews. In March 1943 43 American 'Roughnecks' left New York on the liner Queen Elizabeth, now converted to a troop carrier, surrounded by a convoy of United States destroyers with deck guns at the ready.

Their contract was for one year, and during that time they were billeted in Kelham Hall, chosen mainly because it had two large bathrooms each equipped with four hot showers, that had been installed for a previous military group stationed in the Hall. A partition was built to separate the young oil-field workers from the monks who were already living there.

Between 1939 and 1945 the Eakring and Duke's Wood fields produced over 300,000 tons (some 2,250,000 barrels) of oil from some 170 nodding donkeys - one barrel equals 35 gallons - or one bathfull!

As production declined the Duke's Wood field became uneconomic and it was shut down in November 1965.

In 1991 the then Secretary of State for Energy, John Wakeham, unveiled a 7ft statue of an American oilman at Duke's Wood to commemorate all those who were involved in the discovery, development and operation of the Eakring oilfield.

Known as the Oil Patch Warrior it was created by artist Jay O'Melia from Tulsa, USA. A duplicate memorial stands in Ardmore, Oklahoma.

In May 1987 the Duke's Wood Trail was formally opened, the result of co-operation between BP Petroleum Development Ltd and Nottingham Trust for Nature Conservation, (now known as Nottinghamshire Wildlife Trust). It combined the interest of an area of ancient and secondary woodland, with a site illustrating the pioneering days of one of this country's important industries.

The wood is situated on heavy Keuper clays on a ridge of high ground. It is dominated by oak, ash, hazel and birch. The usual woodland birds can be seen including blackcap, garden warbler and spotted fly catcher in summer. Great spotted woodpecker and jay are regularly seen and hawfinch is a possibility. The ground flora contains primrose, centaury, violet, bluebell, wood anemone, wood sorrel and broad-leaved helleborine. Butterflies include brimstone, gatekeeper and wall brown. Roe deer, fox, stoat and badger do occur, but are rarely seen.

The site is famous for its wildflowers and is classed as a Site of Special Scientific Interest. There is a small site museum and a leaflet guide to the trail markers.

Further information:-
Notts. Wildlife Trust Tel: 0115 958 8242

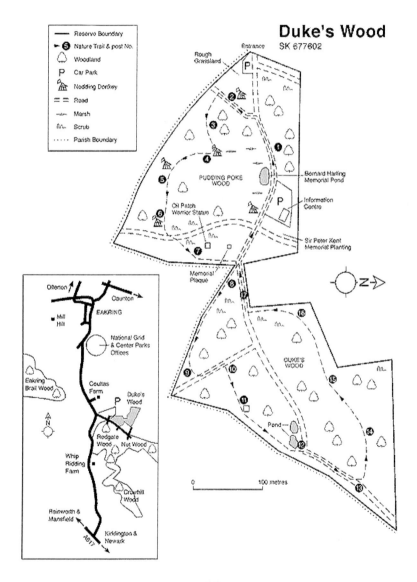

Mompesson's Cross

Eakring

Sk675618

10 miles west Newark A617

signed Eakring

footpath from village

The Rev. William Mompesson is famous as the person who organised the isolation of the Derbyshire village of Eyam during the plague in 1665.

By 1670, still aged only 32, he was an exhausted widower, for his wife Catherine had died only weeks before the colder weather of autumn 1666 finally began to kill off the plague-carrying fleas. His two small children George and Elizabeth, aged 3 and 2 at the outbreak of the plague, had been sent to stay in another part of Derbyshire and they both survived. His patron, Sir George Savile arranged for him to take over the rural church at Eakring, just a few miles from Southwell

On arrival Mompesson preached in the open air, probably because the church had fallen into disrepair, although there is also the legend that the villagers were so fearful of infection that at first he was refused entry into the village. As a result of this he was obliged to live in a small hut in Rufford Park.

Certainly when he was first at Eakring he preached out of doors, standing under a large ash tree, which became known as Pulpit Ash.

His first task was to rebuild and extend the church, adding the side porches, font and pulpit. A year after arriving at Eakring he was appointed by the Archbishop of York to the Prebend of Normanton in

Southwell Minster, where he soon became a most active member of the Chapter. Due to the Civil War only one Prebendal House was available for the Canons and Mompesson became very involved in the rebuilding of the prebendial houses of Southwell.

William Mompesson died at Eakring in 1709 aged 70 and is buried in the church chancel. There is a brass plate and three small windows to his memory.

In 1893 Lord Saville of Rufford Abbey erected this stone cross on the site of the Pulpit Ash, and enduring memorial to a most unassuming but remarkable man.

Halifax Bomber Memorial

Farnsfield SK645554

7 miles east Mansfield A617 signed Farnsfield

On the 6th July 1994, exactly 50 years on, the village church at Farnsfield was overflowing for a special service of remembrance attended by relatives and friends of members of the crew of Halifax Bomber MZ519-LKU.

The plane was on a mission to destroy the VI launch sites and their supply bunkers. These new flying bombs had, over a period of eight weeks, killed 6,184 civilians and seriously injured 18,000 others. Widespread damage was caused and thousands of people were made homeless.

Flying out from RAF Burn in Yorkshire their target was the V1 launch site at Croixdalle. Led by P/O Reginald Parfitt, who had been commissioned just two days, there were altogether seven young men on board.

This daylight attack was highly successful despite moderate flack being encountered by all crews on the run into the target. Heavy anti-aircraft fire was reported over the Dieppe area on the way home.

P/O Parfitt's aircraft was seen to be in trouble with an engine on fire as it passed over Nottingham. It crashed near Farnsfield at 10.25 pm with the loss of all members of the crew.

The bodies of the crew lay overnight in Riddings Farm, close to the spot where the aircraft fell.

Fifty years later a memorial was erected. The stone was quarried in Yorkshire and stands before seven Nottinghamshire oaks, one for each member of the crew.

Two red maple trees flank these - a gift from Canada. Many people and organisations donated the trees to form the remainder of the copse, which has been planted with bulbs and flowers by children from local schools.

Air Marshal Sir John Curtis, who had flown with the same Halifax squadron, unveiled the memorial. The Archdeacon of Nottingham dedicated it, and the RAF paid its own tribute including a fly-past by a wartime Dakota.

In addition, as there were no airworthy Halifax bombers the owners of a model plane were invited to come from Liverpool and join in the fly past. As the plane flew over at about 200 feet, it looked and sounded like the real thing going over at 2000 feet, and many in the large crowd broke into spontaneous applause.

Flintham Museum

SK744458

7 miles south of Newark along A46

This museum shows rural life in Nottinghamshire through the eyes of a village shopkeeper, and is the result of volunteer work on the site since 1990.

The village shop at Flintham closed in 1982, ending 150 years of retailing on the same site. Miss Muriel White, the ex-shopkeeper continued to live there, and one day opened the door to an outbuilding behind the shop which revealed a century of unsold shop stock, with all the relevant documents.

A community project was begun to clean and conserve the finds, and the resulting 2-day exhibition attracted over 700 people. Miss White legally gave the collection to The Flintham Society, and charity status was obtained to open and run a museum to national standards.

An 18th century grade II listed building was bought in Flintham in 1995 to eventually house the museum, but extensive restoration work was necessary before the museum was opened in May 1999.

The building that houses the museum is the result of Robert Hacker's will. He was the owner of Flintham Hall, and when he died in 1729 he had left 12 acres of land in Claythorpe, Lincolnshire, the rent from which would provide a building so that the *poor children* of Flintham could learn to read and *'be instructed in their duty to God and man'.* It was not until 1779 the sufficient money had accrued, and is said to have cost £300. It measured 24x15 feet and was reported to 'hold conveniently 40 scholars'.

Although Hacker's will stated that poor *children* should be educated, only boys attended the school. In 1836, 14 boys aged 7-11 years were selected from the Sunday School to receive free tuition in reading writing and arithmetic.

In 1874 a new school was opened about 80 yards away so the charity school became redundant. However it soon became known as the Reading Room as the charity had invested in a small collection of morally uplifting and general knowledge books.
During World War Two the building was used as a clinic, followed by a boy's club and then a scout hut. The Hacker Trustees sold the building to the Flintham Society in 1991.

The materials used in the old building are typical of those found in many Nottinghamshire villages, with pantiles on the roof and walls of red brick. It is possible that the bricks were made on the site and no two are alike. At the side is a Yorkshire sash window, where the opening section slides sideways.

Flintham Museum was a finalist in the European Museum of the Year 2001 competition, held in Pisa. It was described by the judges as *'possibly the smallest museum visited during the 24 years of the Award's existence.'* Whilst not winning an award the judges' published report stated *'our judges were impressed both by its charm, its regional influence and the professional approach of the volunteers who work tirelessly for it'.*

Flintham Museum open Sundays 2-5pm from April to October - other times by appointment (01636 525111)

www:flintham-museum.org.uk

Admission free - donations welcome

Harley Clock

Harley Gallery, Welbeck

SK551742

5 miles south of Worksop A60

Alan Bennett created this clock in 1995. It was commissioned especially for the Harley Gallery and was three years in the making and is believed to be the only clock in the world with a striking calendar. This can be heard at twelve noon precisely each day as the date is struck on two bells. The Calendar display changes automatically at midnight and takes leap years into account, including the Gregorian 400 year cycle for century years.

One part of the calendar train revolves once in 400 years.

The large weight drives the clock for one month; the smaller weight proves the motive power for the calendar change over and the striking mechanism.

A major feature of the movement is the escapement. It is a modified Mudge gravity type fully jewelled throughout.

The clock is made of glass, steel, brass, rubies, diamond and gold. There is a small mirror on the wall behind the clock to enable visitors to view the mechanism.

The Harley Gallery was built in 1994 on the site of the 19th century gasworks for Welbeck Estate. Thomas of Cuckney founded the Abbey at Welbeck in about 1154 for a colony of canons from Lincolnshire. Following the Dissolution of the Monasteries in 1536, the estate eventually passed to Sir Charles Cavendish, third son of Bess of Hardwick then through successive Dukes of Portland.

The 5th Duke assumed the title in 1854 and much of the present day building, including the addition of a gas works, is due to his designs. At one time between 1500 and 1600 men were employed at one time at Welbeck and £113,000 was paid to a single firm of iron and brass founders for a great variety of works but chiefly for water and gas installations. A number of navvies lived in the grounds and there was a whole encampment of Irish labourers.

The Duke built a roller skating rink and urged his employees to use it, as well as the boats on the lake, for exercise. His consideration even spread to supplying his employees with umbrellas and donkeys, to enable them to travel comfortably to work.

On the 25th September 1875 the Duke of Portland was 75. About 800 children from local schools, all of which were supported by the Duke, processed through the village, with banners and flags, up to a large tent hired for the occasion. There the children and widows enjoyed cake, bread and butter and tea, after which the public were admitted. Dancing followed until 11 pm.

The following year the Duke was ill in London, so there were no demonstrations at Welbeck, except that the workforce left somewhat earlier than usual and

'also for each person there was a liberal allowance of good old ale, in which the health of the nobleman was drunk right heartily..'

The 5th Duke of Portland died on the 6th December 1879 and was buried simply as was his father, who had stipulated that no more than one pound was to be spent on his funeral.

Relaxation Mediation Centre

SK825723

'Pure Land' N. Clifton

13 miles north of Newark A1133

This Japanese Garden is the life work of a Japanese monk The second son of a noodle factory owner, he was free to enter monastic life, and change his name to Maitreya. After obtaining an MA degree in Buddhist Theology he went travelling in Thailand, India and Nepal.

Through the invitation of a friend he came to England where he stayed in various centres and universities round the country teaching and lecturing. It was whilst staying in Teversal in Nottingham he came across this property for sale in North Clifton. It consisted of a 300-year-old farmhouse along with two acres of weed-infested wasteland.

His main aim was to create a garden that was to provide a peaceful, beautiful area for guests and visitors to enjoy. So in 1980 he began the process, despite the fact that he had no previous gardening experience.

He missed the hilly and mountainous scenery of Japan and so started to create his own in miniature. The earth dug out by the JCB in order to create the pond was heaped roughly into 'hills' to be shaped by hand later. The large stones came mostly from a quarry in Derby, a pagoda was built from scrap metal found in a shed while the plump Koi carp cost £10 a dozen from a pet shop.

The winding paths are built to confuse the devil!

Many plants were given by friends and villagers, mostly familiar British variety but shaped and pruned to look Oriental. Local farmers helped with the task of moving the large stones.

A Japanese Tea House has been built for tea ceremony use.

The garden also has a small open-air refreshment area for light snacks, tea and the monk's own homemade scones!

As well as the garden Maitreya also runs a Meditation Centre offering individual tuition, group relaxation as well as audio tapes.

For more information: Tel: 01777 228567

Castle Colonnade

Central Nottingham

SK395567

The Duke of Newcastle rebuilt Nottingham Castle, and it was completed in 1679. He recycled the stone from the old Castle, and had several feet of rock cut away to form a platform for the new house. The last residents quit the building in 1829, and in 1878 the Prince and Princess of Wales opened the first provincial Museum of Fine Art in Nottingham Castle. Mr T.C. Hine, the town's architect, redesigned the entrance to incorporate a colonnade (and public toilets.)

Funded by the National Lottery a new slate and cobble floor design has been created incorporating poems by local people.

Within the colonnade stand several memorials to local dignitaries, including one to Quakers William and Mary Howitt.

They married in1821 and William opened a chemist's shop in Nottingham, but both he and Mary dreamt of becoming writers. Three years later when Byron's funeral procession passed on its way to burial at Hucknall, the pair laid their hands on the coffin, hoping some of his literary skill would pass to them.

Mary wrote 'The Book of Seasons' that received excellent reviews and ran into many editions.

In 1831 Dorothy and William Wordsworth were staying at an inn opposite the Howitts' house on Parliament Street when Dorothy was taken ill with lumbago. She moved in with the Howitts for recuperation. Then William published 'History of Priestcraft' which caused a considerable sensation. Its denunciation, particularly by the Quakers, greatly increased its popularity and it quickly had to be reprinted. Almost overnight William became famous in Nottingham, and soon had been elected an Alderman.

In 1840 William published *'The Rural Life of England'* which included fascinating chapters on such places as Hardwick Hall, Newstead Abbey and Sherwood Forest.

In 1836 the pair left Nottingham, but wherever they lived they continued to write prodigiously. Mary became the first person to

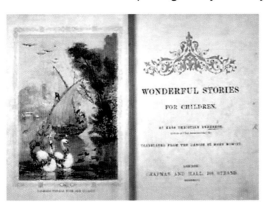

translate from the Danish some of Hans Andersen's stories. Andersen was delighted with the result as he was very keen to be known in England, as he already was in other countries. He said he regarded Mary as a sister and begged her to translate all his tales. This, to her lasting regret, she refused to do, being too busy with other work. Hans Andersen then visited England and stayed with Howitts, but they found him a difficult and moody guest and were quite glad when he left.

By now the couple lived in St John's Wood, London and living nearby was Charles Dickens who became a close friend. When he launched a new weekly journal - *'Household Words'* he begged them to contribute, which they did for many years.

Mary was an ardent supporter of the anti-slavery movement. She also helped organise a petition of some 30,000 signatures urging the passing of a Bill which would give married women control over their property.

The bas-relief within the colonnade came about in 1900 when it was proposed to Nottingham Council that six monuments be erected for a cost of £1,800. Mary has her arm round William who said of her *"she was destined to be my best friend, truest companion and wife."*

Beside them stands a bust to Lord Byron.

D.H. Lawrence Statue

Nottingham University Campus
SK386544

A6005 Nottingham Ring Road towards Beeston
Campus signed

David Herbert Lawrence was born in 1885 in Eastwood, Nottingham. He won a scholarship to Nottingham High School, and by 1902 had returned to Eastwood as a pupil teacher. Four years later he took up a teacher training scholarship at University College Nottingham, and his two years as a student were critical, both in terms of his personal development and his career as a writer.

During this period he not only wrote poetry, but also completed the second draft of his first novel, and wrote his first short stories. One of these, *A Prelude* marked his first appearance in print, in the *Nottinghamshire Guardian,* December 1907.

Lawrence's circle of friends and acquaintances expanded at University College. It was here that he met Louie Burrows, to whom he became engaged, and others on whom he would later draw in creating fictional characters. Most significantly, it was at University College that he met Professor Ernest Weekley, Professor of Modern Languages. In 1912, he was to elope with Weekley's wife, Frieda.

This statue is the work of British sculptor, Diana Thomson FRBS and was unveiled by members of the Lawrence family on 18 June, 1994. It is located at the highest point of the campus, outside the Law & Social Sciences Building, to the rear of The Hallward Library. It shows Lawrence in outdoor clothing and with bare feet, as though he is striding through the countryside. Gentle cradled in his hands is a vivid blue gentian. It was inspired by Lawrence's poem 'Bavarian Gentians' which was written towards the end of his life and first published in *Last Poems* in 1932.

In fact Lawrence had been suffering from tuberculosis for many years, and by this stage was virtually bedridden. It is thought friends came to visit and bought him a gentian, which was put on a nearby dresser. Gazing at it Lawrence wrote

Reach me a gentian, give me a torch!
Let me guide myself with the blue, forked torch of this flower...

He goes on to relate the flower to Persephone, a daughter of Zeus and Demeter, who was abducted by Pluto, King of Hades. For six months of the year she must reign as Queen alongside Pluto but is allowed to return to the surface for the other six. Persephone carries the flower torch-like into the underground to light her way to Pluto's chambers.

Lawrence says it is Death which has come, and the flower acts as a guide into the "sightless realm." Like Persephone there will be springtime rebirth, for although he body may be dead, his consciousness arises again each time his words are read.

The DH Lawrence Collections at the University of Nottingham Library today form one of the major international research resources for the study of the writer. The School of English Studies offers an MA in D.H. Lawrence and the Modern Age. In addition, the University's D.H. Lawrence Research Centre, established in 1991 to serve the interest of Lawrence scholars from all over the world, hosts a programme of activities.

More information can be obtained from

Department of Manuscripts & Special Collections
Hallward Library
University of Nottingham
University Park Nottingham NG7 2RD

Tel 0115 951 4565
Web site: http://mss.library.nottingham.ac.uk/

Pumping Station
Papplewick SK585522
7 miles from Nottingham 7 miles from Mansfield A60
signed Pumping Station

Between 1720 and 1830 the population of Nottingham rose from 10,000 to 50,000 largely due to the development of the Framework Knitting and Lace Industry, the extra population being housed within the bounds of the medieval town. The water supply from the river Leen became inadequate and was heavily contaminated with sewage and industrial wastes. Epidemics of cholera and typhoid occurred, and although the cause was not fully understood, the appalling condition of the water supply was thought to be a contributor.

In 1880, responsibility for water supply passed to the Nottingham Corporation Water Department whose engineer, Mr Ogle Tarbotton submitted an urgent report, the result of which was the construction of Papplewick Pumping Station. It contains two 140 hp. James Watt rotative Beam Engines and a second Mapperley Reservoir both brought into operation in 1884. These were driven by six hand fired Lancashire boilers, insulated and covered in brickwork. About 2,000 tons of coal was used each year and all the coal and ash was moved by hand.

Papplewick ceased regular operation in 1969 but remained on standby until 1972. A Trust was then formed to preserve this outstanding example of ornate Victorian architecture, first as a static exhibit, but now as one of the finest working period waterworks in Europe.

Papplewick Pumping Station was built to a fixed price contract, but not all the money was used, so the surplus £15,00 was spent on elaborate decoration, including stain glass windows, brass decoration and unique terracotta. Ibis were chosen as they appear when the Nile

is in flood, and represent a period of abundance and fertility.

Papplewick Pumping Station is scheduled as an ancient monument, the engine house, boiler house and workshop are listed Grade II* whilst the gardens are included in the English Heritage Register of Parks & Gardens. These contain a fine collection of hollies. The planting is predominately evergreen with either shiny or needle-like foliage, which was able to withstand the effect of the soot from the 120 ft high chimney.

The Pumping Station is open in the afternoons with the machinery static, and in steam Bank Holiday Sundays and Mondays. For details:

www.papplewickpumpingstation.co.uk
Tel: 0115 963 2938

Shireoaks Marina

SK555815

4 miles north west Worksop A57

The former Shireoaks Colliery site near Worksop has been developed into a new marina with a capacity for 60 craft. With a water space of approximately 4500 sq.metres it offers 24-hour visitor mooring, residential mooring or long-term mooring, for both narrowboat and cruisers. Funded and supervised by Nottinghamshire County Council, in partnership with East Midlands Development Agency, the aim was to develop the derelict colliery to produce residential land, restaurant development and the marina.

Henry Pelham-Clinton, Fifth Duke of Newcastle, who lived at Clumber Park was responsible for digging the pit in Shireoaks. The Duke was a strong churchman and he was concerned for the spiritual condition of the miners and their families. He commissioned his architect Mr T.C. Hine to build a church *'for my colliers, who badly want it.'*

The Chesterfield Canal, which runs through Shireoaks, stretches over 46 miles, and is one of the country's oldest canals being officially opened in 1777. The waterways most illustrious cargo was the stone used to rebuild the Houses of Parliament after the great fire in 1834. It came from the quarry at North Anston near Worksop.

Shireoaks has also been designated the start of a major cycle path by Sustrans. Route 6 will enable cyclists to travel from there to Long Eaton in Derbyshire.

Part of the improved canal towpath near Shireoaks has been surfaced with red shale. This is burnt colliery waste, and is popular with the British Horse Society as more than a fifth of the 68 kilometres of Route 6 in Nottinghamshire is on bridleways.

Dovecote at Sibthorpe

SK765454

8 miles south Newark off A46

This impressive structure was built over 650 years ago and is one of 22 dovecotes to be found in Nottinghamshire. It is both the earliest, being built about 1342, and the largest in the county.

Dovecotes are believed to have been developed by the Romans as a source of food. Certainly pigeons were easy to keep and cost very little once the dovecote was built as they found their own food, feeding indiscriminately on everyone's crops, often making them unpopular with local farmers.

Not only did they provide eggs and fresh meat the year round, but a large dovecote was an expression of stature and wealth. The pigeon dung was also used as a manure to enrich the soil and in the tanning of leather. It was also used to bleach laundry and in the manufacture of saltpetre for gunpowder. Medicinally both the pigeon and its dung were considered important.

An important consideration in the construction of a dovecote was the safekeeping of the birds both from vermin and from poachers. Rats are able to climb so rat ledges, a projection encircling the building were constructed. To stop poachers carrying out large hampers full of birds entry was by way of a small single door. At Sibthorpe this only measures 3'9" (1.3 m) high by 2'3" (0.7m) wide.

33

Inside the structure the walls are honeycombed with over a thousand nesting places in 28 tiers floor to roof. Each small square aperture has a landing slab and a nesting chamber precisely formed in the stonework, and today looks as perfect now as when it was built .

Originally the dovecote formed part a collegiate complex which was built in connection with the foundation of a college of priests in 1335. St Peter's Church has a 13th century tower and a 14th century chancel.

The decline in pigeon keeping resulted from changes in farming methods. Gradually the idea spread of keeping cattle and sheep through the winter so that fresh meat was available all year round.

Sibthorpe Dovecote is a Grade I Listed building and the surrounding fields are a Scheduled Ancient Monument.

Swan & Waterfowl Sanctuary

Reg Taylor's Garden Centre SK707549

2 miles from Southwell towards Normanton

The Sanctuary began in the 1960s when there was just one lake given over as a refuge for sick and injured swans. Since that time it has expanded continually until it now comprises 6 lakes, set in 9 acres of landscaped, tended grounds - including boathouses, bridges and thousands of trees, shrubs and bulbs.

The latest phase in the expansion of the Sanctuary began in the early 1990s as more and more species of waterfowl were added from all over the world.

A breeding programme was established, rearing birds to interest zoos and collectors - both in the UK and abroad. Emphasis was particularly turned towards the breeding and protection of endangered species. With the rapid growth in human population around the world, many wetland areas are coming under strain from pollution and the encroachment of towns and cities. Wildlife in those areas comes under great pressure too - and the Sanctuary is trying to make a contribution towards helping to redress the balance.

The Swan population has not been neglected either; with the improvements in veterinary and after-care facilities, they are better able than ever to look after injured swans, and work towards returning them to the wild.

The Sanctuary is completely privately owned and receives no funding of any sort from local or national Government. To help fund their continuing work, there is a small charge for visiting the Sanctuary.

Reg Taylor's Garden Centre lies less than a mile from the market town of Southwell. It has been family run for over 50 years. Reg Taylor began as a nurseryman, and today the family remain very active growers, with nurseries occupying a total of 50 acres, both adjacent to the Garden Centre and at two other sites.

On site there is a Restaurant offering home cooked food for Breakfast, Lunch and Afternoon Tea. Booking is recommended especially for Sunday Lunch, Christmas Fayre (December) and special occasions such as Mothering Sunday and Easter.

For Restaurant reservations:

Tel 01636 813184 (Ext. 225)

The Blue Room

Thoresby Hall
SK639712

3 miles north of Ollerton
on the A614
Signed Warners Hotel

The present Thoresby Hall was commenced in 1865 when Sydney, 3rd Earl Manvers and his half-French countess, Georgine, built a new house 500 hundred yards further from the lake. The architect was Anthony Salvin, renown for his great medieval halls, and mixture of classical styles in the other State Rooms.

Following the death of the widowed 6th Countess at the age of 94 in 1984, Thoresby was put up for sale, but twice purchasers went bankrupt. In the 1990s it was declined by the National Trust and put on the English Heritage 'at risk' register.

In 1998 Warner's Holiday Ltd bought Thoresby Hall. By then it had been empty for nearly 10 years. The roof was leaking; wet and dry rot had attacked the fabric of the building, and woodworm and death-watch beetle were in evidence. In less than a year, working within the restraints of a Grade I Listed Building, and a commercial budget, the skilled craftspeople from the small firm of Herbert Read had to restore the four State Rooms to their former glory. The firm had worked in most of the royal Palaces, including restoration work at Windsor Castle, as well as Churches, Cathedrals and other Warner Hotels.

The beautiful ceilings, such a feature in the State Rooms, had been almost destroyed by water. However, wherever possible the original paintwork was consolidated and carefully cleaned with only those

areas that had been lost being repainted. The result is in the Blue Room the vast majority of what is seen today is the original pain scheme applied nearly 150 years ago.

Thoresby Hall contains a fine collection of beautiful marble fire surrounds, with those in the Blue Room being a fine example. The matching pair depicts the four seasons and are the result of much

restorative work, for one had been stolen, the other smashed. Painstakingly the broker pieces were collected and reassembled, and lost elements reproduced to match salvaged sections.

The Blue Room gets its name from the striking padded silk wall hanging which is said to have been woven to match furniture designed for Casanova. However when Warners took over the fabric was rotten and hung in tatters. Small sections of the original fabric that had been protected by things like light switches were used as a colour match. The new fabric was produced using stencils taken from the original material. Although slightly thicker than the original and a little coarser, in order to provide adequate protection against fire, it still enriches the overall decorative scheme in this stunning room.

The Blue Room is now used as an a la carte restaurant, which is open to the public.
Tel 01623 821000.

Millennium Window

St Swithin's Church
Wellow

SK6716662

2 miles east of Ollerton A616

The parishioners of Wellow had no difficulty in deciding the theme for their Millennium Window, as only four other permanent maypoles remain in the whole of England!

The existence of a Wellow Maypole can be traced back at least as far as 1856. Then in 1860 a new pole had to be erected as the old one had been sawn down during a drinking spree a few weeks earlier. To commemorate Queen Victoria's Jubilee in 1887, a new pole was given by Sir John Savile, which had three crosspieces near its summit, painted spiral decoration and a seat around the base. In 1923, the Jubilee Maypole was replaced by Lord Savile and this pole lasted until 1937 when it was found to be unsafe and cut down from 30 feet to 20 feet. In 1949, this pole was finally chopped down for safety reasons and in 1950 a new pole was bought from the Rufford Estate. This pole lasted until 1966 when it was damaged by storm, and was taken down and sold for firewood.

Another pole of larch was obtained from Thoresby Estate, but on finding it had not been properly seasoned, it was declared unsafe by Nottinghamshire County Council and, in 1976 it was chopped down to half size. That year the dancing took place round the reduced pole.

Later in 1976 the remainder of the pole was taken down, and in 1977 with the help of a heritage year grant, a three section 60 foot tubular steel pole was purchased from Abacus Engineering of Sutton in Ashfield.

This present pole is decorated with three cross-pieces with metal crown shapes at each end, and surmounting the pole is a weathervane made by a local engineer.

Originally celebrations took place on May Day itself, but in recent years they have been held on Spring Bank Holiday Monday. A principal part of the proceedings is the crowning of the May Queen who is chosen by a secret ballot of villagers held earlier in the year. The girls have to be between 12 and 17 years of age.

During the festivities the retiring Queen crowns the new Queen and then she takes her place on the May Throne to watch the maypole dancing. Four maids of honour who are selected according to the results of the poll accompany her. There is also a retinue that includes the herald, bugle blower, posy bearers, train bearers and a crown bearer.

Wellow has another claim to fame, as it is one of only two villages in Nottinghamshire with a large central green. Its triangular shape is very unusual. Cattle were brought here for safety from wild animals and thieves. It is known that markets were held on the green in 1267 and 1330.

In 1207 the monks of Rufford Abbey paid 10 marks (£100) to build houses and lay hedges in Wellow. However, in 1209 the men of the village were fined 20 marks for pulling them down!

For more information about Wellow Maypole Celebrations:-
Contact the Tourist Info Centre
Tel: 01623 824545

The Church of All Saints

West Markham SK7227228

2 miles north of Tuxford B1164

This fine little church almost ceased to exist for when the 4th Duke of Newcastle built his family mausoleum it unusually incorporated a church. Strangely he wrote in his diary for the 25th February 1824 *Took Mr Smirke* (a leading architect of the day) *to look at the new situation which I propose for the site of the new church where I intend to have the family cemetery. I have fixed upon West Markham where there is now a very bad church. I mean to remove it to a central position between West Markham, Milton and Bevercotes. Afterwards I shall remove the Parsonage house and place it near the Church.'* A faculty from the Archbishop of York dated 10th May 1824 permitted the old church of All Saints to be demolished.

In 1832 the Duke wrote in his diary

'I have looked at the old church with Mr E. Dawkins, the vicar, and we agree that it will be best to pull down great parts of the old church, reduce it in size and rebuild the bad parts making it fit for the performance of funerals.'

It is unknown why the work was not carried out, but it was indeed fortunate for it is an important ancient church, but for more than a hundred years the church, whilst still consecrated, remained unused. A group of parishioners led by their vicar, the Rev G. Crookenden, in 1930 embarked upon a programme of restoration.

During the war all building and non-essential renovations had to cease, but by 1949 a Consistory Court ruled that All Saints was once again to be a Parish Church. The Bishop of Southwell conducted the inaugurate service on October 30th 1949.

The south door is considered to be one of the oldest in the county dating from the 14th century at least. Inside are examples of Saxon and early Norman brickwork, and unusual hop vine carvings. The font is dated 'not later than 1090' and is lined with lead. It would originally have had a lid, which could be locked against witchcraft. As it was only filled and blessed at Easter, end of the year christening must have been pretty polluted! The base is carved with eight priests under arcades, one with a chalice and two with books.

The burial slabs in the floor of the chancel are graves of previous vicars and family. Several are post 1678 when Charles II passed the Wool Acts which stated that

'No corpse of any person shall be buried in any shirt, shift, sheet or shroud or anything whatsoever, made or mingled with flax, hemp, silk, hair, gold or silver, or in any stuff or thing other than what is made of sheeps wool only'.

It was an attempt to protect the industry from the importation of cotton, and was in force for 150 years. Also by Law the Clergy had to keep records of these burials. At Markham the largest burial slab is estimated to weigh about two tons.

According to the excellent Church Guide Book,

'The old oak benches are Elizabethan. It is recorded in 1584 nine men were prosecuted for playing football in the churchyard one Sunday. The game ended in a fight, one man being killed. The guilty were sentenced to make penance and undergo corporal punishment. One, a landowner, was allowed to commute his penalty to a fine, the money to provide a seat 'in which parishioners might take the sacrament'.

This little Church is a fine example of a congregation working together to restore and revive a near-derelict building, resulting in a beautiful and active Parish church.

The Guide Book can be purchased from the Church

Woodthorpe Tropical House SK435585

2 miles north of City Centre off A60

The Woodthorpe Nursery Tropical House was opened in 1995 as part of the redevelopment and modernisation of the Woodthorpe Grange Nursery. Great emphasis was placed on environmentally friendly products, both in the construction of the greenhouses and in the peat-free loam used in the beds. Pests such as glasshouse whitefly are controlled using a tiny parasitic wasp, and sachets containing their eggs and larvae can be seen hanging from some plants. These insects have no harmful effects on the plants or the other beneficial creatures living within the Tropical House.

The plants grown within the Tropical House are from the more exotic regions of the world that would not grow here without indoor protection. Many the plants produce familiar everyday products and are a main source of income to the country of origin, for example olives from Asia Minor, rubber from India and bananas from The Antilles.

There is also a small pond created with rock quarried from Bulwell stone. It contains approximately 30 platinum Koi carp that were approximately three inches long when the House was opened in 1996, but are now quite a substantial size.

The Tropical House is open Tuesday to Friday 9.30 to 3pm in winter and an hour longer in summer. It is also open in the mornings at week-ends, but is always closed on Mondays. Admission is free with good wheelchair access.

The Tropical House is situated at the top of Woodthorpe Park, an area of some 40 acres, which is always open for public recreation. In addition to grassed areas for picnics and play, there are two grass

football pitches, as well as Nottingham's only Pitch and Putt facility. The park is also used for Travelling Fairgrounds and special Fun Days.

In addition there are formal flower beds cared for by the City of Nottingham's Recreation Dept. Their nurseries within the grounds of the Park provide all the flowers and foliage within the City, including the traffic islands, planter and hanging baskets.